THRIVING *with* ADHD
WORKBOOK FOR TEENS

THRIVING *with* ADHD

WORKBOOK *for* TEENS

IMPROVE FOCUS, GET ORGANIZED, *and* SUCCEED

ALLISON TYLER, LCSW

ILLUSTRATIONS BY LAURA BREILING

ROCKRIDGE
PRESS

For general information on our other products and services or to obtain technical support, please contact our Customer Care Department within the United States at (866) 744-2665, or outside the United States at (510) 253-0500.

Rockridge Press publishes its books in a variety of electronic and print formats. Some content that appears in print may not be available in electronic books, and vice versa.

TRADEMARKS: Rockridge Press and the Rockridge Press logo are trademarks or registered trademarks of Callisto Media Inc. and/or its affiliates, in the United States and other countries, and may not be used without written permission. All other trademarks are the property of their respective owners. Rockridge Press is not associated with any product or vendor mentioned in this book.

Interior & Cover Designer: Jay Dea
Art Producer: Janice Ackerman
Editor: Lia Ottaviano
Production Editor: Matthew Burnett
Custom Illustrations: © 2019 Laura Breiling

ISBN: Print 978-1-64152-617-3
eBook: 978-1-64152-618-0
R0

To my favorite ADHD muse, my dearest Callum.
You will always be my inspiration to learn more,
do more, and advocate for those with ADHD.

Your curiosity, creativity, and sensitivity to the
world around you will bring you to great places.

Never stop building, never stop asking questions,
and never stop seeing the bright side.

CONTENTS

LETTER *to* TEENS

Imagine this: You wake up late (you forgot to set your alarm), you jump out of bed realizing (yikes!) you have only ten minutes to get ready! As you head to your closet, your phone flashes. Just a quick look—you chime in on the late-night group text that you missed and scroll Insta and Snapchat to see what everyone's been up to. Before you know it, five minutes have gone by . . . and now you really have to race to make it to the bus on time. You get dressed, run to the bathroom, and go to find your backpack. Ugh . . . where did you leave your backpack again? Dining room table? No. Oh, right: You decided to do your homework in the basement last night. You run to the basement, grab your backpack, shove your books and papers inside, and book it to the front door just in time to see the back of the bus as it turns off your street. Missed it. AGAIN. Sound familiar? Perhaps it was really easy for you to imagine this scene. Perhaps this scene was what happened this morning for you.

If you are a teen with ADHD and you struggle with time management, organization, prioritizing, and negative thinking, then this book is for you. This book is also for you if you want to learn what is great about ADHD, what untapped strengths you may have but have not yet recognized, or how to tackle and finally solve the problems that you seem to encounter over and over again.

My name is Allison Tyler, and I've been working as a psychotherapist with children, adults, and teenagers with ADHD for more than 16 years. I'm also a parent of a child with ADHD. I understand the struggles that ADHD can present, but I also know the hidden joys and wonders of the ADHD brain.

With ADHD, you may at times feel alone, different, overwhelmed, frustrated, depressed, or anxious, but I'm here to tell you that you (and all these feelings) are normal. I'm going to teach you how to discover and harness your hidden talents, feed your growing inventiveness, and tame your unruly doubts with interactive exercises, quizzes, and practical advice.

In this book, you will learn about the different types of ADHD. I will break down the executive function skills (the ability to plan and prioritize, organize, control impulses and emotions, think logically, and self-monitor, for example) and I will guide you through the process of figuring out which of these skills you should focus on to achieve better balance in your life. Using a blend of motivational, cognitive-behavioral, and mindfulness techniques, I will also teach you specific approaches and strategies to help build your working memory, organizational and prioritization skills, and help quiet your anxiety.

Finally, I'll guide you through the choppy friendship waters, throw you some lifelines, and point out new ways you can think about living your best ADHD life. By the end of this book, you should know your ADHD self better, understand which skills you need to work on and practice, and what your strengths and superpowers are. ADHD doesn't have to stand in the way of fun or success—ADHD is what makes you who you are, and the more you understand about it, the closer you will be to achieving your goals.

PART ONE

THE TRUTH ABOUT ADHD

FIRST THINGS FIRST:

Let's get the basics out of the way. After reading this section, you will learn what ADHD is and what ADHD isn't, and you will also understand the different types of ADHD. ADHD comes in all shapes and sizes and right here is where you will start your custom fitting. Why is this important? By understanding what your ADHD is and how it affects you, you will be better equipped to integrate new skills and strategies into your life. You will also learn what those pesky executive function skills are and how they affect your life.

Next, I'll dispel some myths about ADHD and give you the straight facts and statistics. After all, you are not alone. Many people across the world have ADHD.

Finally, we will discuss the realities of dealing with school and how you can get help when you feel overwhelmed. The good news is that there are many strategies to get you back on track when you feel lost or stressed out. There are also some tricks, hacks, and routines that can be easily integrated into your lifestyle. Some of the skills I'm going to teach you may feel weird when you first try them, but keep an open mind and stick with it. The more you practice, the better you will get and the more comfortable you will feel implementing the skills in your daily life. I will be here to guide you each step of the way. **So, let's jump right in . . .**

All About ADHD

What is ADHD? ADHD, which stands for Attention Deficit Hyperactivity Disorder, is a neurodevelopmental condition that causes a person to have difficulty staying focused and/or to be hyperactive or impulsive. Very simply, having ADHD means that your brain is wired slightly differently. Scientists do not yet know for sure what causes ADHD. There is a genetic link to ADHD, and we'll talk more about that later, however some research also shows a correlation to some environmental factors such as brain injury, premature birth or low birth weight, or early childhood exposure to pesticides or lead. We do know that ADHD is *not* caused by bad parenting, sugar consumption, family stress, trauma, or watching too much TV or screen time, according to CHADD (Children and Adults with Attention-Deficit/Hyperactivity Disorder).

The symptoms of ADHD generally start to become apparent during your childhood when your body is growing. Specifically, there is an area of your brain right behind your forehead called the frontal lobe. This part of your brain is responsible for many functions, including problem-solving, memory, delaying gratification, attention, impulse control, and more. Imagine your frontal lobe is a busy eight-lane highway, with some of the cars going super fast, some going super slow, and some constantly changing lanes. The traffic in this intersection of your brain can sometimes cause information to get delayed, congested, or confused. This can lead to issues with learning, listening, focusing, remembering information, reading social cues, and feeling in control of your body and emotions.

ADHD TREATMENT

Treatment for ADHD can vary. Some choose to take medication. The most common medications fall under the stimulant category, and the way they help is by increasing the level of the chemicals dopamine and norepinephrine in your brain. These chemicals help the brain increase its ability to focus and maintain attention and alertness.

The choice of whether or not to take medication is a very personal one. Some people do fine without it, whereas others feel as though medication has made a huge difference in their lives. It's important to discuss medication with your doctor and your parents to figure out if the medication route is right for you.

While you may recognize some of these symptoms in your own life, ADHD should only be diagnosed by a specialist doctor such as a psychiatrist or a developmental pediatrician. These specialists make their diagnosis by doing an interview with you, collecting information from your school and a parent questionnaire, and conducting various tests.

ID Your ADHD

Now let's dig into the types of ADHD. There are three main types.

Check off the symptoms that apply to you.

Type 1: Inattentive (The Dreamer)

- ☐ Forgetful
- ☐ Easily distracted
- ☐ Short attention span with everyday activities
- ☐ Difficulty sustaining attention
- ☐ Trouble listening
- ☐ Struggles to follow tasks that require instructions
- ☐ Difficulty with organization
- ☐ Makes careless mistakes and appears to not pay close attention to details
- ☐ Avoidance or dislike of tasks that involve sustained mental effort

Type 2: Hyperactive (The Motor)

- ☐ Constantly fidgeting and squirming
- ☐ Difficulty engaging in activities quietly
- ☐ Excessive talking
- ☐ Interrupting and blurting out answers before a question is finished
- ☐ Difficulty waiting or taking turns
- ☐ Difficulty remaining seated

Type 3: Combined (The Dreamy Motor)

☐ Forgetful

☐ Easily distracted

☐ Short attention span with everyday activities

☐ Difficulty sustaining attention

☐ Trouble listening

☐ Struggles to follow tasks that require instructions

☐ Difficulty with organization

☐ Makes careless mistakes and appears to not pay
close attention to details

☐ Avoidance or dislike of tasks that involve sustained
mental effort

☐ Constantly fidgeting and squirming

☐ Difficulty engaging in activities quietly

☐ Excessive talking

☐ Interrupting and blurting out answers before a
question is finished

☐ Difficulty waiting or taking turns

☐ Difficulty remaining seated

Here are the Stats on Your ADHD Brain

More than **7 percent** of children worldwide have ADHD, and **3.2 percent** of adults worldwide are considered to have ADHD. That makes ADHD pretty commonplace globally. Just think: In your town, in your neighborhood, and all across the world, there are other teens dealing with the same ADHD symptoms as you.

In the United States, **10.2 percent** of children (on average) have a diagnosis of ADHD.

In the United States, **6.2 percent** of girls are diagnosed with ADHD.

In the United States, **14 percent** of boys are diagnosed with ADHD.

While the research shows that boys have a higher rate of being diagnosed, it also shows that women get diagnosed more in adulthood. Some research also shows that certain behavior, especially impulse control and the ability to focus, is detected more readily in boys than in girls. So, it's important to know that ADHD may present slightly differently in boys and girls.

While there currently aren't a lot of statistics available on transgender children and ADHD, research is being done and the results are slowly starting to emerge. Nonbinary kids may fall into either category.

IF THE GENES FIT . . .

You may notice that you aren't the only one in your family with ADHD traits. Maybe your dad struggles to be on time or your brother seems to be constantly in motion. ADHD is considered to be hereditary, so it wouldn't be unusual for your mom, dad, sister, or brother to also have the condition. While a specific ADHD gene has not yet been identified, scientists do believe that at least one or two genes are responsible for the condition. The good news is that you might be able to use this common family denominator to better understand each other.

Here are the stats on your genes (according to Barkley 2015):

You have a **57 percent** chance of having ADHD if your parent has it.

You have a **32 percent** chance of having ADHD if your sibling has it.

If you have an identical twin with ADHD, you have a **70 to 80 percent** chance of also having ADHD.

ADHD in Real Life

Sometimes it's hard to look in the mirror and recognize all of your ADHD traits. However, knowing which symptoms of ADHD affect you is important so you can better home in on which strategies you can use to overcome your symptoms. So now that you know a bit more about ADHD, read the following descriptions of real-life scenarios and try to figure out if you can tell which type of ADHD each teen has. It may be helpful to read through these scenarios with someone you trust. Do you see yourself in any of these descriptions?

Eden is in chemistry class. The teacher is going over the table of periodic elements. It's a beautiful morning and Eden looks out the window and sees the lawnmowers cutting the grass outside her school. She watches intently, almost mesmerized as the lawnmower makes neat stripes down the lawn. The next thing she knows, her teacher is in front of her waving his hand in front of her face trying to get her attention. **Which type of ADHD is Eden?**

Alex is SO excited to be cast in the school musical. This year his school is doing *Little Shop of Horrors* and Alex has landed a speaking role. It's the first rehearsal/read-through of the play. Alex can't stop bouncing his foot, and as soon as the director asks the cast to sit down, Alex immediately asks the director several questions about his role. The director asks him to hold questions until the read-through is over, but Alex can't resist and interrupts several times to give other cast members high-fives, getting up each time. By the end of the rehearsal, the director has had to take Alex aside to discuss play-rehearsal etiquette. **Which type of ADHD is Alex?**

It's lunchtime and **Casey's** best friend, Anne, is having major girl-friend drama. Anne wants to tell Casey what happened and get some advice. Casey agrees to sit down with Anne for a conversation but runs into her lacrosse teammates in the cafeteria line. They start discussing the upcoming game against their longtime rival. Casey chimes in while checking her phone and sees a reminder that she has a history test next period. She runs out of the cafeteria, completely forgetting about Anne and leaving her teammates looking bewildered. **Which type of ADHD is Casey?**

What the Heck is Executive Function?

Have you ever walked into your bedroom and forgotten why you went in there? Do you have a hard time keeping track of your homework? When dealing with problems with friends, do you feel like you sometimes overreact or make impulsive decisions that you later regret? These are all examples of how deficits in executive function skills affect your life.

Executive function skills are a set of skills your brain uses to help you organize and access information and emotions. They enable you to plan and prioritize, organize, control impulses, control emotions, think flexibly, initiate tasks, access working memory, and self-monitor. Most people with ADHD have deficits in some or all of these executive function skills. The good news is that there are tricks and strategies that you can learn and practice to help strengthen these skills. In this book, I will help you identify which skills you need to work on and the best strategies to practice them.

What is Working Memory?

Your brain has three different types of memory: long-term, short-term, and working. Long-term memory is information that has been stored and filed away. Examples of long-term memory are your address, important birthdays, phone numbers, etc. Short-term memory is information that your brain stores for a short period of time but is not converted into long-term memory. Examples of short-term memory are a list of items to buy at the grocery store, daily homework lists, or what you had for breakfast three weeks ago. Working memory is the ability to manipulate short- and long-term memory, such as doing mental math or remembering verbal directions from a teacher and applying them to your work during class. Why is working memory important?

Working memory helps you to do the following tasks:

- mental math
- daily organization
- problem-solving
- responding appropriately to questions asked in class
- remembering and carrying out instructions

Think of working memory as your internal clipboard, where you can copy and save information so you can access it when needed. For people with ADHD, the clipboard isn't available, or it disappears and you lose the information needed to complete the process. Read on for tips and tricks to help strengthen your working memory.

EF AF!

Check out the different ways that deficits in executive function skills can affect all aspects of your life.

- Losing your keys (again and again)
- Overreacting to a problem with a friend
- Keeping your papers in a mess in your backpack
- Losing your cool when plans change suddenly
- Being shocked to learn that you failed a test
- Forgetting about play practice
- Being consistently late to appointments or classes
- Forgetting about plans you made with your best friend
- Feeling totally overwhelmed by a research project and not knowing where to begin
- Underestimating the amount of time it will take to do homework
- Not thinking about an assignment after you receive it back graded
- Regretting the comment you impulsively made on Snapchat
- Not knowing how to prioritize. For example, even though you have a test tomorrow that you haven't studied for, you decide to work on your research paper that is not due for another three weeks.
- Rushing through a list of chores your parents gave you so you can meet your friends at the mall.

How EF Plays Out in Real Time

Now that you know more about executive function skills, let's take a look at several examples of how deficits in these skills play out in everyday situations. Read through the following scenarios and think about whether any of the situations sound familiar. Do you relate to or see yourself in any of the scenarios? One of the most important executive functions is the ability to self-reflect. That means the ability to look at yourself, examine the way that you performed academically or socially, and think critically about it. Self-reflecting is sort of like looking in your own rearview mirror: It provides the ability to see where you need to make improvements, changes, or ask for help or support. After we self-reflect, we can then ask ourselves, when I do this next time, how would I do it differently so I can achieve a different result?

Self-reflection is the skill that will help you make changes in your lifestyle and habits. As we work together through this workbook, I will ask you to practice this skill in different ways. By the end of the workbook, self-reflection will have become easier and easier, and you'll have a better understanding of how self-reflection and the lessons you learn from it can set you up for future success.

James has to read *Of Mice and Men* for language arts class, and he has to have finished reading the book by Monday's class. The assignment was given three weeks ago. James finally opens the book to start reading at 10 p.m. on the Sunday night before it is due.

Cheryl's mother reminded her three times that she has to leave early for a work meeting and she needs Cheryl to be ready to go at 7:30 a.m. At 7:28, Cheryl charges around the house trying to get everything ready for school. Her mother is in the car furiously honking the horn when Cheryl rushes out to the driveway at 7:38 a.m.

Julia just got her Spanish quiz back. It's another 70. She remembered all the words and meanings, but she misspelled them and got points taken off. This is the third quiz she's had this semester with misspelled words. When she gets the quiz back, she shoves it in her backpack with no plans to ever think of it again.

Gwen is at dance class and her dance teacher is on her case. She seems to be criticizing everything Gwen does. By the end of class, Gwen is fed up. She lashes out at her teacher, calling her a name, and tells her that she is quitting the dance team.

MYTHS/TRUTHS ABOUT ADHD

Myth: Having ADHD means I am terrible at focusing/paying attention to everything.

Truth: Many teens with ADHD have the unique ability to "hyper-focus" when they are involved in something they find interesting or enjoyable. This ability can be harnessed and redirected with targeted practice and by learning new brain-based skills.

Myth: I take a stimulant that helps me concentrate at school, so I don't need any other help.

Truth: Stimulants help reduce ADHD symptoms in up to 80 percent of people who take them. Stimulants increase the release of neurotransmitters, which helps reduce congestion in your brain's communication pathways (remember the highway example from earlier?). However, most people with ADHD have deficits in executive functioning skills such as organization, time management, and prioritizing and usually need support to learn specific skills to achieve a healthy rebalance.

Myth: ADHD makes everything difficult for me—school, friends, my family, and sports. I will never be successful.

Truth: ADHD can make aspects of life challenging; however, most people with ADHD learn to capitalize on their strengths as they mature and go on to have happy and successful lives and careers.

Myth: My mind is racing. I'm constantly thinking about what's coming next and I feel like I'm all over the place. This is what ADHD feels like.

Truth: Having a diagnosis of ADHD puts you at higher risk of having anxiety. In fact, studies show that 30 percent of children and adolescents with ADHD suffer from anxiety. Learning mindfulness techniques and thinking-targeted strategies to slow down and redirect your thoughts can be extremely helpful.

ADHD in School and Life

It may seem like ADHD is wreaking havoc on all aspects of your life, especially school. School may be the place where you have received a lot of negative feedback in the past from teachers (and maybe even from yourself), but I'm here to tell you that you can change this. Practicing some of the techniques that you will learn in this book can really help change not only the way others react to you, but hopefully the way that you view yourself as a student. It's also important to think about when to tell people about your diagnosis. Having an open dialogue about your challenges with those who can help you is a productive way to problem-solve. You don't need to broadcast it to every person you encounter; however, sharing it with the key people in your life—such as teachers, coaches, bosses, and close friends—can help them understand you and make problem-solving easier. Here's an example to illustrate how sharing your ADHD diagnosis appropriately can help you be more successful.

Belle, who is in 8th grade, was recently diagnosed with ADHD. This year, she was constantly late for her language arts class and got multiple detentions for handing in her homework late or incomplete. The constant negative feedback began to wear on her and she started to feel frustrated. Today, she is attending her first IEP (individualized education plan) meeting at school. This is the meeting where the accommodations being made to help her at school are going to be discussed. At the meeting, Belle learns that she will be given extra time for all her tests. All her homework assignments will be available for her to read in an online portal (so she doesn't have to worry about forgetting what they are) and her teachers will use a color-coding system to help her stay organized. Belle's guidance counselor will meet with her weekly to review her workload and check in with her about how she is scheduling time for her assignments. Belle leaves the meeting feeling so relieved and excited about the rest of the school year. She understands that she has some support and she now knows the resources available to her.

ACCOMMODATION STATION: IEP VS. 504

What's an accommodation? Accommodations are changes in education designed to remove barriers to learning for students who may need a bit of extra help in their studies. These accommodations are normally given via two routes: the Individuals with Disability Act (IDEA) or Section 504 of the Rehabilitation Act. Depending on which route best meets your needs, you will either have an IEP (individualized education plan) or a 504 plan. Here are some examples of common accommodations for teens with ADHD.

- Extra time for tests
- Preferential seating (closer to the teacher or the whiteboard)
- All homework assignments to be communicated and accessible on Google Classroom
- Assistance in breaking down longer assignments into short-term tasks
- Color-coding tasks
- Reduced or modified homework assignments
- Tutoring or assistance with organization

If you feel like you may benefit from an accommodation but you do not currently have one, you should talk to your parents first. Be specific about what you feel you may need that would help you in the classroom. Usually, receiving an accommodation requires one (or several) meetings with your teachers and specialists, such as a learning disability teaching consultant, who may conduct educational assessments to figure out how to best help you.

How to Talk about ADHD to Other People

You might feel ashamed or embarrassed to tell people about your ADHD, or it may feel as though you are completely exposing yourself. It's common to feel this way, but luckily the world is changing and schools and workplaces are much better equipped for a neurodiverse population. (Neurodiverse: a fancy way of saying that all people's brains are different.) Many schools and workplaces are normalizing the act of making accommodations for people with ADHD.

Check out the following example, which illustrates how sharing your diagnosis with a work supervisor can help improve your outcomes for success at work.

Bridgette just got a job working at the ice skate rental shop at the local hockey rink. She is super excited but nervous about making mistakes. On her first day, her supervisor trains her how to use the cash register, reviews the organization of the skates, and explains how the staff schedule works. Bridgette takes notes in her phone to help her remember all the new information. After the orientation, her supervisor asks if she has any questions. Bridgette says no but explains that she has ADHD, which means that she sometimes needs an extra reminder or needs a little extra time and practice to learn new routines. Her supervisor thanks her for sharing and says his son also has ADHD. He suggests taking a picture of the staff schedule, which changes each week, so she can text it to herself. He tells her he will also email her all the new training materials so she can store them digitally to review at home.

WHAT TO DO WHEN SHARING MY DIAGNOSIS DOESN'T HELP?

It's great when you have a supportive supervisor who is sympathetic to your unique situation. But what should you do when you have a teacher or boss who doesn't seem to care about your ADHD?

- Seek outside help.
- Speak to your parents, guidance counselor, or another work supervisor.
- Ask for guidance and support.
- Remind them that by sharing your diagnosis you are trying to do the best job possible.

Unfortunately, not everyone is going to be understanding, so it's important to seek out the support of people who are. If your boss isn't helpful, you should speak to your boss's supervisor. Similarly, if your teacher isn't supportive of you, you should document what happened and go to your guidance counselor or principal. It may feel intimidating or daunting to do this, so make sure to ask your parents for help. Just remember that standing up for yourself and advocating for what you need sometimes takes time and repetition until you get the right response. It may be helpful to practice what you want to say or roleplay with a trusted friend or parent, so that you feel comfortable getting your point across.

Thriving with ADHD

What I really want you to get out of this book is that ADHD is not a condition that you have to suffer through or simply survive. ADHD makes you different and unique in ways that can help you thrive and live an awesome, fulfilling life. By introducing some positive new habits, skills, and strategies into your life, you can begin to see ADHD through a different lens. If you currently use harmful strategies to deal with ADHD—such as avoidance, procrastination, negative self-talk, or self-medication—know that there are better, healthier ways to embrace ADHD as part of your life. You now have a whole book of resources to turn to for help and guidance.

Check out this list of actors, scientists, inventors, entrepreneurs, athletes, and politicians who all lead successful lives with ADHD:

- Michael Phelps
- Adam Levine
- Justin Timberlake
- Simone Biles
- will.i.am
- Bill Gates
- James Carville
- Katherine Ellison
- Jason Kidd
- Stephen Hawking
- Ellen Page
- Dean Kamen
- Audra McDonald
- Cammi Granato
- David Blaine

HOW TO GET HELP

Sometimes ADHD isn't the only thing you're dealing with as a teenager. It's more common for teens with ADHD to also have anxiety, depression, or a mood disorder. Being a teen in today's world is stressful, and if you feel like you are dealing with sadness or excessive worrying or you feel like your moods are out of control, it may be time to consider asking for some help. Talk to your parents or your school counselor about how you feel and consider getting professional help from a therapist. Talking about your feelings can help you feel less isolated and alone and is the first step to feeling better.

You Can Be Your Own CEO

Think about yourself as the CEO of YOU, Inc. All the different parts of your life are the departments you oversee: school, friends, sports, family, hobbies. At times, it can be overwhelming to try to keep all of these departments running smoothly. However, as you get to know yourself better, understand your strengths and weaknesses, and learn new skills, you will start to feel more and more confident about being the leader of your own life.

In the following sections, I'm going to cover a wide range of strategies and exercises for dealing with ADHD. Some of these strategies and exercises may require you to think differently, to take a deep look at yourself, and to be honest about some of your strengths and weaknesses as both a student and a friend. We will cover how to get organized, how to prioritize your homework and calendar, and how to motivate yourself when you have difficulty initiating a task. We will tackle anxiety and negative self-talk strategies, friend problems, how to relax and get your brain to sloooow down, and how to harness your hyperfocus. We will touch on some good writing strategies, study habits, how to minimize distractions, and how to create an ideal workplace for homework and studying.

There are a few things you will need to help you get the most out of this workbook:

- a set of different-colored highlighters
- Post-it or sticky notes
- a set of index cards

At the end of each section, you will notice a spot for you to post your "sticky note self-reflection." I encourage you to put your sticky there and jot down a few key ideas, words, or thoughts that stick out to you about what you've just read. I'll help you with some thought-provoking prompts to get you started. Doing this will help the ideas you've just learned stay in your long-term memory and also help you think about how the ideas apply to your life.

So now you know a bit more about ADHD, what it looks like and what it doesn't look like, and most importantly, you know a bit more about how ADHD affects you. Now let's move on to learning some strategies to help you at school.

PART TWO

ADHD IN SCHOOL

HERE'S THE GOOD NEWS: Schools provide many more tools and resources to students with ADHD now than they did years ago. Educators know so much more about ADHD and are much better equipped to help you in the classroom. But what do you do when you leave the classroom? There's a lot to keep in mind: homework, studying, staying organized . . . Don't worry, I got you. Let's get started on the key strategies to make you a success story at school.

1. Build on Your Strengths and Understand your Weaknesses

Everyone has subjects they excel at in school and areas that are really challenging or frustrating. Knowing your strengths can help you build your confidence. Identifying your weaknesses can help you locate specific tools and strategies to address what's challenging for you.

> **Kristin** just got back her third D on a social studies quiz. It's so frustrating. She studies for the quizzes by reading over her notes diligently, but she notices that she can't keep track of dates. She always forgets them on the tests and it's really bringing down her scores.

Think of a class you do well in. What are some strengths you have in that class? What do you enjoy about it?

Think of a class that's difficult for you. What are some weaknesses you have in that class? What mistakes do you tend to make? Does your experience sound like Kristin's?

Here are some common strengths students have:

Having creative ideas

Ability to write clearly and communicate ideas concisely

Working quickly and efficiently

Showing good leadership in group work

Ability to multitask easily

Here are some common weaknesses students have:

Making careless mistakes

Poor attention to detail

Failure to fully follow through ideas

Difficulty finishing to completion

Difficulty retaining information that isn't "interesting"

Using a highlighter, identify any strengths or weaknesses that you have in your classes.

Sticky Note Self-Reflection

Write down the strengths and weaknesses you highlighted on your sticky note.

2. Start Uploading to Your Internal YouTube Channel

Madeleine gets nervous every time she has to take a test. It doesn't matter how much she studies or how prepared she is. The day of the test she starts thinking the absolute worst: "I'm going to fail this test. I'm not going to remember anything. This is going to be a disaster." And then she starts feeling awful—her stomach hurts and she begins to panic as she walks into the classroom.

Have you ever noticed the power your thoughts have over your feelings?

If thinking that she is going to fail a test is powerful enough to make Madeleine's stomach hurt, imagine what could happen if she shifted her thoughts to be positive instead of negative. A great way to try this is through visualization. Visualization means accessing a memory or visual image in your head and watching it as you would watch a movie or a show. Think of a positive memory relating to your worry. For example, if you're worried about a test, think of a time when you felt prepared for a test, approached it with confidence, and aced it. If you're worried about giving a speech, think of a time you spoke in public and the audience reacted positively or clapped for you. If you have trouble visualizing a school-related positive memory, think of any positive thought or memory that makes you feel calm and happy. Some examples might be a place you visited on vacation, spending time at a beach or a park, a birthday party with friends and family, a sports play you are proud of, or a theater performance you were in.

Sticky Note Self-Reflection

Write down three positive memories that you can recall whenever you feel anxious about a test or a presentation. Keep them in your memory bank and replay them in your head as though you are watching your own YouTube channel of positive vibes.

3. Keys, Wallet, Phone . . . Keys, Wallet, Phone

Before **Corey** leaves the house, she utters this phrase to herself several times to make sure she doesn't forget essential items. After a while, it becomes part of her routine and just starts to happen automatically. As she prepares to leave the house, the phrase starts playing in her head: keys, wallet, phone; keys, wallet, phone . . .

Make a list of the most important things you need to take with you each morning when you leave for school. Your list can include the basics—like keys, wallet, and phone—and also your homework, a signed permission slip, supplies for a class project, etc. List them here.

Now make up a mnemonic device to help you remember. You can sing it to a tune you'll remember or even make a rap that rhymes. Have you ever created a mnemonic device to help yourself remember things?

This is one that almost everyone knows:

30 days has September, April, June, and November

All the rest have 31

Except for February, my dear one

It has 28 and that is fine

Except in a Leap year and then it's 29

Sticky Note Self-Reflection

Write your mnemonic device for remembering your morning essentials.

4. Workspace Edit Part 1

Izzy sits down to start her homework and is immediately distracted by things around her, from the smell of dinner cooking downstairs to the sound of the TV playing in her sister's room to the ticking of the clock on the wall.

Sound familiar?

The first step to getting in the zone to get stuff done is to look at your immediate work environment. There are a few key things to consider when it comes to your surroundings: where your workspace is (choosing a quiet space with a door you can close is ideal), what's right in front of you, what's next to you, and what you can hear/smell/see that may distract you.

Take a look at Izzy's set-up and identify any potential distractions that will prevent her from having a productive work environment. Use one color of highlighter to indicate the distractions you think she should remove.

Sticky Note Self-Reflection

Write down three potential distractions you can think of right now that you can "edit" out of your workspace.

5. Workspace Edit Part 2

Now that you've edited your workspace to minimize distractions, let's talk about adding a couple of key tools that may help you stay focused and work better. Following is a list of tools that can really help. You may not have all of these tools at home and that's okay. Once you've completed this exercise by highlighting the items to add and writing them down on your sticky note self-reflection at the end of this section, make sure to discuss the list with your parents and determine which tools you may already have and which tools you have their permission to borrow or purchase. Use a highlighter to identify the tools you think will best help you.

Noise-cancelling headphones (use these if you are very noise-sensitive and need to block out exterior noise in order to study or write)

Ear plugs (use these if you need complete silence to study or write)

Oil diffuser with a calming or energizing scent, such as lavender, citrus, or bergamot

Speaker to play background noise or music (try soft classical music, which has been shown in studies to help ADHD brains!)

A **timer** to help you stay focused on the task at hand (especially if the timer on your phone or computer makes it too easy for you to get distracted by texts or social media)

Sticky Note Self-Reflection

Write down the items and tools you have highlighted.

6. Play Your Organization Card

Jonathan's family always jokes that he would lose his head if it weren't attached to his neck. He misplaces things, forgets important dates, and loses track of time so often that he is frequently late for plans with friends or forgets about the plans altogether.

Getting (and staying) organized can be especially difficult when you have ADHD. Being organized does not come naturally to everyone, and it can feel overwhelming if you're not sure how to get organized. However, starting some regular organizational routines can really help you stay on top of things.

Here's a strategy that may help take some of the guesswork out of organization for you. First let's figure out the specific areas of your life that need more consistent organizing. The examples we're going to use are your backpack, bedroom, and calendar, but you may be able to think of more—such as your closet, phone, and email.

Take out an index card for each area and label the top of the card. Then write three specific tasks you should do on a weekly basis to keep each area organized. Once a week (preferably at the same time each week), pull out your cards and complete the three items. Pro tip: Help make this a routine by setting a reminder on your phone or creating a weekly reminder using Google Remind Me. Don't worry if you forget one week; you can always pick up where you left off, but try to make a habit of doing the three tasks each and every week so you don't get behind.

Backpack

Take everything out and throw out any garbage or unneeded items.

Place all loose papers in the folders they belong in.

Put away any items I don't need to take to school.

Bedroom

Place all dirty laundry in the hamper and put clean clothes away.

Make bed.

Put shoes back into closet.

Calendar

Set a reminder for all homework assignment due dates for the week.

Add any changes to sports practices/games.

Check family schedule to add in any doctor appointments or events.

Sticky Note Self-Reflection

Choose a time and day of the week for your weekly organization roundup. Write it on your Sticky Note. Put it into your calendar and create a reminder (such as in Google Calendar or Remind Me).

7. What's Your Study Style?

Kay has a final exam coming up in her AP physics class. She's noticed that her friends can study for hours at a time in the library, but she struggles to pay attention after 20 minutes of reviewing her notes. She notices that her mind starts to wander, she can't remember what she just read, and she starts to move around restlessly. It's so frustrating for her when everyone else seems to have no problem focusing and absorbing the material.

We all have different ways of taking in information. The way people study can vary vastly from person to person. If you're having a hard time staying on task while studying or concentrating, try this: The next time you have to study or concentrate on something, set a timer. As soon as you start becoming distracted or losing focus, check your timer to see how much time has passed. Maybe it was 25 minutes, 13 minutes, or even 7 minutes. Take a break for 3 minutes, and then, set the timer for the amount of time you recorded. When the timer goes off, take another 3-minute break.

As you practice this, slowly increase the time in 1- to 2-minute increments each time. See if you can slowly build your focus and concentration. Continue to take 3-minute breaks between study sessions. Don't get discouraged if you feel you aren't improving right away, and remember that some days will be harder than others. Success and improvement rarely happen in a straight line. As long as you keep trying, you're improving.

Studies show that regularly scheduled breaks can help ADHD brains stay focused and fresh. Working or studying in short bursts can be a very effective way of accomplishing tasks, so don't get frustrated if you can't sit and concentrate for really long periods of time. What you are doing is finding the best way for your brain to work or study.

Sticky Note Self-Reflection

Put a reminder in your calendar for the next time you need to study or work on an assignment. Try the preceding exercise with a timer and see how you do. Use the Sticky Note to keep track of your efforts at focused time, or reflect on your experience.

8. Find Your Brakes for Break Time

Maurice has a Spanish quiz tomorrow. He starts reviewing his vocabulary words on Quizlet. After 10 minutes, he notices his mind is starting to drift and he isn't remembering the definitions. It's time for a break. Maurice grabs his phone and Googles the best new fishing poles for lake bass. The next thing he knows, 45 minutes have gone by. He's yawning and has fallen down a deep internet search vortex.

Has this ever happened to you?

Let's talk about the best activities for your brain when you decide it's time for a break. The activities below are healthy and encourage your brain to stay focused and organized.

- Taking a short walk outside (use a timer if you think you may take too long a walk)
- Doing a few yoga poses
- Eating a healthy snack
- Petting your dog/cat/pet
- Drawing/coloring (use a timer)
- Listening to music (try classical)
- Reading a chapter or two of a good book
- Playing a short card game
- Listening to a podcast
- Exercising or dancing for a few minutes
- Meditating (try a short 1- to 3-minute meditation)
- Organizing your workspace

Use your highlighter to identify the activities that interest you for when you need to take a homework or study break.

Here's a list of activities to avoid:

Anything involving Google, social media, or the internet

Playing video games

Texting with friends

Watching TV (Netflix, Hulu, etc.)

Online shopping

E-mailing

Eating junk food

Sticky Note Self-Reflection

Write down the activities you highlighted from the healthy activities list and put them into practice the next time you take a homework or study break.

9. Color Code Your Classes

Hudson opens up his backpack to find his algebra worksheet that he needs to finish for tomorrow. Inside, he finds a bunch of crumpled handouts and an overstuffed notebook that he uses for all his class notes. He begins the tedious process of going through each pocket to try to find where he put his worksheet.

Sorting and sifting through information can be challenging for people with ADHD. It's related to the executive function task of prioritizing. Studies show that visually organizing information by color can help ADHD brains make clear associations. For example, using a different colored pen or pencil to take notes for each subject may help you better organize the information in your brain and make it easier to recall during a test. It can also help you locate information when scanning visually.

Using colors to stay organized is a proven strategy for ADHD. There are a couple of different ways you can do this. You can assign a color to each of your classes and get correspondingly colored folders to hold all the homework and papers for each class. Additionally, if you use a digital calendar or reminder system, use the same designated class color to highlight due dates for each class. If you use a physical calendar or planner, use the same color sticky notes to highlight due dates for each class.

Sticky Note Self-Reflection

Write down each of your classes and use your highlighters to assign a color to each class.

10. Writing Can Be Your New Best Friend

Teagan has to write a persuasive five-paragraph essay for her language arts class. She has a lot to say but she doesn't know where to start. Her ideas are all over the place and seem jumbled in her head. Every time she has to write she feels anxious and frustrated. She thinks, "Will it always be like this?" She sits at her computer, staring at the blank Word document and willing the ideas to come onto the page, but nothing happens. It's going to be a very long night.

Writing with ADHD can be challenging because you are relying on several executive functions to work in harmony. Sometimes it can feel like your brain is playing a game of tug-of-war. But don't worry! There are some proven tricks and strategies to get the ideas flowing and help you tap into your inner writer.

Use a **graphic organizer.** Graphic organizers give you a frame for your ideas. They can help you visualize where you want ideas to go and how they fit together.

Use **sticky notes** to brainstorm. Write each idea down on a sticky note. Once you have a bunch, you can start sorting them with your graphic organizer.

There are some great **dictation tools** you can use, such as Dragon Anywhere, which transcribes your spoken words into a document on your computer. Sometimes speaking aloud is a great way to get your ideas flowing.

Use a **mind map.** This is a great way to help direct your idea flow when it feels like you are all over the place. The idea is not to try to control your ideas but to get them all down in one place so you can later sort them into categories by similarities. See the following sample STORY mind map.

Create a **checklist** using the rubric or outline given by your teacher. Once you are finished, make sure to proofread your work for errors and ask someone (a parent/friend/teacher) to read your first draft. Writing is a process, and getting feedback is a helpful step to reaching a great final draft.

Sticky Note Self-Reflection

Write down two writing tools that seem interesting to you. Set a reminder on your calendar to try them for your next writing assignment.

11. Harness Your Hyperfocus

Jo notices that when it comes to certain things, especially things he enjoys, such as photography and anime, he can focus for hours and hours. But when it comes to something he dislikes or that seems boring, such as studying Spanish vocabulary, his mind does everything it can to veer off track.

Hyperfocus, or the ability to intensely concentrate on something, can be an elusive skill to harness. Sometimes it seems like hyperfocus happens out of the blue and you find yourself doing something highly detail-oriented, such as organizing your jewelry box; hyperfocus may also stop or start with no warning.

Here's a trick to try to tame your hyperfocus and aim it toward your schoolwork.

Set a timer for 3 minutes. Look at the following picture and try to find three of the items in the arrows to the left of the picture.

three mice

smiley face button

rain boots

Try to incorporate this exercise several times a week for a few minutes at a time, to work on increasing your hyperfocus. You can do this by completing seek-and-find exercises (such as Where's Waldo?), using an app such as Elevate, or playing a memory card game.

Sticky Note Self-Reflection

Jot down the remInders you'll add to your calendar to practice your hyperfocus exercise.

12. Write On, Dude

Ollie has a really difficult time keeping track of dates in his head. He has a test coming up on World War II, and in order to keep the information fresh in his mind, he writes down all the important dates over and over again. Sometimes he does it on sticky notes, sometimes on flash cards, and sometimes on his dry erase board. He even makes himself sample tests with blank fill-ins.

Here's a study technique with a proven track record to help you retain information when you are studying. Write it down—again and again and again. This may sound simple, but studies show that writing down information with a pen and paper helps seal the information into your memory. Here are a few different ways to do this:

1. **Use notecards** to make flashcards with vocabulary words, important dates, or other information.

2. **Use sticky notes** to remind yourself of important information—stick them to your notebook, bathroom mirror, computer screen, etc.

3. **Use color-coded pens** or scented pens.

4. **Make a small illustration** or cartoon next to each study point to help you visualize that piece of information.

5. **Create rhymes** or songs to help you remember study points.

Sticky Note Self-Reflection

Write down a study strategy that you plan to use during your next study session. Write it in your calendar and don't forget to add a reminder!

13. Goal Time

Before you sit down to work on your homework, write a paper, or study for your physics quiz, take a moment to write down a specific, realistic goal that you want to achieve. Write it on a sticky note and put it somewhere you cannot miss, such as on your laptop, on your notebook, or on your phone to dissuade you from getting off task.

The key is to make the goal realistic and reasonable for your timeframe. So instead of "study for Spanish quiz," you might write "memorize 10 vocabulary words." Or instead of "finish trigonometry homework," you might write "complete 4 problems on the worksheet." Not only will this help you manage your time better, but by breaking down tasks that initially may seem overwhelming into smaller chunks, they will be much more manageable and less intimidating.

Dinorah has set aside 30-minute chunks this evening to get her homework done. She has a lot to do, including writing a paper for her English class and studying for a Latin test, and she is feeling overwhelmed. She'd like to break down her big tasks into smaller, more specific and attainable goals, but she isn't sure where to start.

In the following chart, using the previous example as a model, write a smaller, more specific goal in the right-hand column to correspond with each big task in the left-hand column. For example, if your big task is to work on your English paper that's due in three weeks, a smaller goal might be to write a draft of the introduction.

Big Task	Smaller, More Specific Task
Work on English paper	Write a draft of the introduction
Read language arts assignment	
Finish algebra worksheet	
Study for Latin	
Work on chemistry project	

Sticky Note Self-Reflection

Check out an assignment you have coming up and try breaking it down into smaller, specific goals. Add them to your calendar and set reminders for completing each one in a timely manner.

14. Straight Talk about Your Phone/There's an App for That

Michael just sat down at his desk to write an article assignment for his language arts class. He is in a good headspace and starts getting some great ideas down using a mind map. Ten minutes in, his phone tweets and he sees that his best friend texted him; two minutes later, another buzz and he sees that his brother just tagged him on Twitter; and 30 seconds after that his friend from across the country Snapchats him. The next thing he knows, he has picked up his phone to catch up on what he missed. By the time he tries to get back to work, his head is swimming and he feels unfocused and scattered.

The great thing about technology is that there is technology to help us deal with the distractions caused by our technology. Follow? There are some great apps out there that can help keep you on track and minimize distractions that otherwise might easily and very quickly take you off the road to accomplishing your goals, both big and small. I've tested many of them and I have a few favorites that I recommend.

OFFTIME: This app blocks other apps on your phone and you can sync it across devices. You can designate the amount of time you want to set the block for.

Cold Turkey: This one allows you to block websites and apps that you know are time-sucks. Cold Turkey is very strict. Once you start, there is no turning it off or turning back. Not for the faint of social media heart.

Freedom: With this app, you can pretty much block anything on any device. It also allows you to schedule your blocks in advance for when you know you need to be extra focused—for example, when exams are looming.

RescueTime: RescueTime blocks distracting sites and tracks productivity. It also tracks how you spend your digital time, so this may be a great app to get started with if you want to see how much time you really spend on certain apps, websurfing, reading reddit, etc.

Hocus Focus: This app is for blocking one window at a time on a Mac. It acts as a menu bar so you can stay focused on one thing at a time. It's great for those who find that they lose time when they start to "work" on their laptop.

Sticky Note Self-Reflection

Write down an app you would like to try the next time you need to be distraction-free; put a reminder in your calendar to try it out.

15. Motivation Station

Reina finds that when it comes to school subjects she particularly dislikes, she cannot motivate herself to start homework. For example, tonight she has to write up her chemistry lab. Chemistry lab is her least favorite class and she has been dreading the homework all day. Whenever she tries to sit down to do it, she finds that she would rather do almost anything else, even cleaning her room or doing other less urgent homework.

It's hard to find motivation when it isn't there to begin with. When it comes to a particular task you are dreading, a good rule is to ask yourself if you are procrastinating (putting something off). If the answer is yes, you may want to try one of the following hacks to help you find your motivation mojo.

1. **Pair a like with a dislike.** If you really dislike a particular type of homework, it can seem like torture in your head. In order to minimize those negative feelings, try doing the hated homework along with something you enjoy, such as listening to an interesting podcast, sitting outside, or diffusing a favorite essential oil.

2. **Promise yourself a reward.** We are all motivated by rewards. Sometimes you have to dangle the carrot for yourself in order to get an unpleasant task done. Write down on a sticky note a small reward that you can give yourself after you finish the task; ideas might include a favorite snack, FaceTiming with a friend, or watching an episode of your favorite show (only use this one if you aren't planning to do more work after you finish the dreaded task). Place your reward sticky somewhere you can see it easily from where you're working.

3. **Break it down.** Some tasks require a lot of mental energy, and we dread them because we know how taxing they are. If you are trying to accomplish a task that completely overwhelms you, try breaking it into two or three smaller tasks. For example, "complete 10 trig problems" is a task that's much easier to digest than completing a full page of 35 problems.

4. **Cover it up.** Speaking of a full page of problems, looking at a huge piece of work can create feelings of anxiety. If this happens to you, use a black folder or large piece of paper to cover the work you aren't currently focusing on. This visually blocks out information that's not pertinent to the task at hand and keeps your eyes on only what you are working on.

5. **Your future self thanks you.** Visualization is a powerful tool. Imagine how happy and accomplished you will feel after you have completed the task you've been putting off; let that feeling motivate you to get it done.

Sticky Note Self-Reflection

Write down a strategy you would like to try the next time you need to find some motivation. Put the sticky note somewhere you will see it in your workstation.

16. Working Backward is Best

Fiona has a research paper for history due in a month. Looking at the calendar, choose from the list of tasks and assign two appropriate mini tasks that she can do each week that will help her write her paper. Work backward from the due date. Don't forget about holidays and soccer games that Fiona also needs to add. The paper is due on November 30.

NOVEMBER 2020

S	M	T	W	T	F	S
1	2	3	4	5	6	7
8	9	10	11	12	13	14
15	16	17	18	19	20	21
22	23	24	25	26 Thanksgiving	27	28
29	30					

List of tasks

- Mindmap/brainstorm ideas
- Soccer game on Nov 15
- Gather evidence/quotes on notecards
- Complete first half of paper outline
- Complete paper outline
- Write first two pages
- Write second two pages
- Soccer game on Nov 5
- Write final two pages
- Proofread/complete bibliography
- Final draft done
- Soccer game on Nov 10

Sticky Note Self-Reflection

Write down what you have coming up in the next month. Have you scheduled everything in your calendar?

I hope you have been able to identify your strengths and weaknesses and learned some new study strategies and organizational and planning skills. Remember that your skills will keep evolving the more you practice them, so hang on to your sticky note self-reflections and refer back to them often. Schedule some time in your calendar to review once a month what you have learned.

Now that we've got school covered, let's take a dive into how ADHD affects you out in the big wide world. There's lots for us to discuss about friends, drama, work, parents, stress, and learning how to relax.

PART THREE

ADHD IN THE WORLD

NOW THAT WE'VE EXPLORED ADHD at school and learned some new tricks for managing your schedule, study habits, and environment, let's take a look at how ADHD affects your life outside of school. You may feel like ADHD takes over everything and that it's hard to know what to do when specific issues come up, such as arguments with friends, staying organized at home, managing conflicts, and maintaining a healthy view of yourself. Just as we did with school, let's dive into your world one issue at a time and cover some new territory to help you realize that you are in the driver's seat.

1. Can't We All Just Get Along?

Willa just got into a huge fight with her best friend, Angela. Willa was venting to Angela about not making it onto the varsity softball team. Willa felt like she worked really hard and was disappointed that she was one of the only juniors not to make it. Angela told her that she shouldn't have skipped two of the practices that were offered and that Willa needs to commit herself more and take things more seriously. Willa feels like she got slapped in the face. What happened to being a supportive friend? Whose side is Angela on? Willa's initial reaction is to stop speaking to Angela and to let all their friends know what a jerk Angela is being.

Conflicts with friends are tough and can be hard to navigate, period. But when you factor in ADHD, it can get a little more complicated. You may feel things intensely, or feel very strongly about your side of the story, and it may be difficult for you to hear someone else's point of view. Conversely, you may feel that you get treated unfairly because of your ADHD or that your friends minimize your feelings or discount what you have to say. Whatever the case, here are some key strategies to keep in mind when you are in a conflict with a friend.

1. **Allow some time to cool off.** It's always good to give yourself (and your friend) some time before you react. If this is difficult, make sure you take the Impulsivity Pulse Quiz (page 75) for some additional tools that may help. Take a walk, listen to some music, or talk to someone impartial.

2. **Evaluate why you are upset.** Once you have had some time to calm down, think about what is most upsetting to you about the conflict. Do you feel disrespected? Were your feelings not recognized? Was your trust broken?

3. **Schedule a time to talk in person.** It can be really tempting to try to resolve a conflict via text, but there are so many ways that texts can further complicate a disagreement. You can misread the tone, write something impulsively that you would never actually say to someone's face, or put something in writing that

you would hate someone else to see. It's important to remember that anything you communicate digitally—whether it's a Facebook status, Instagram post, or text message—can be forwarded to someone else. If you wouldn't want your mom to read it, don't text it. If you wouldn't want your teacher to see it, don't Snapchat it.

4. **Focus on how you feel and what you need.** Try using "I" statements to focus on how you feel. For example, "I feel hurt that you pointed out what I did wrong. I was really sad that I didn't make varsity and I just wanted you to listen to me and let me vent."

5. **Allow the other person to speak.** This can be challenging to do when you're deep in your own hurt feelings, but make sure you listen to what your friend has to say and make sure they feel heard in the same way you want to feel heard. Reflect what they say back to them: "So, you're saying that you were only trying to be helpful when you pointed out that I missed two practices."

6. **Problem-solve for the future.** Conflicts are opportunities to make changes and grow. Talk to your friend about shifts that you will both make so you can better understand each other when another conflict arises.

Sticky Note Self-Reflection

Which of these strategies would you like to try the next time you have friend drama? Write it down.

2.

Are You Listening to Me?

Take this quiz to figure out if you are a listening pro or if you need to brush up on your skills.

It's lunchtime and two of your friends are telling you about their teacher's epic meltdown after no one participated in the class discussion in world history. Which sounds most like you?

a. As they talk, you notice your crush get up to buy a bottle of water and you immediately start daydreaming about going on a date with them.

b. You nod your head and laugh at all the right places, but when the story ends, you immediately change the subject to what you've been wanting to talk about ever since you sat down.

c. Your friend does the best impression of their world history teacher. You ask her to repeat it, and when they finish the story you exclaim, "I cannot believe that happened. That must have been so crazy to watch!"

Your soccer team just got completely obliterated on the field. After the game, your coach calls the whole team in for a pep talk and some feedback. As he talks, you

a. Replay all of your mistakes in your head, as well as those of your teammates. You can't even hear him talking.

b. Look up at your coach every few minutes so he thinks you are listening, but you're actually thinking about what you're going to have for dinner tonight.

c. Make eye contact with your coach. Even though it's hard to hear, he's making some good points that will hopefully help the team avoid similar mistakes in the future.

On the ride home from school, your mother goes over a few things she needs you to do while she is on a conference call this evening. They include walking the dog, turning on the oven to 375°F degrees for dinner at 4:30 p.m., and setting the table.

The chances you will remember to do all three are

a. Awwww, look at that adorable puppy!

b. Fifty-fifty. I'll probably remember to take the dog out because she scratches at the back door.

c. Easy-peasy, lemon squeezy. I set reminders on my phone so I won't forget the tasks Mom asked me to do tonight.

If you answered mostly As, your listening skills could use a little reboot. Try these strategies to tone up your weak listening areas.

1. **Make and maintain eye contact.** People with ADHD can sometimes forget to make eye contact and this can result in poor listening ability (not to mention the person you're talking to will probably think you're not interested in what they have to say, and that never feels good). Remember to meet the eyes of the person you are listening to at least once or twice per minute.

2. **Use reflective listening.** Pretend you are a recorder bouncing back the language you are hearing back to the speaker. You don't have to do this word for word, but in your own words reflect back to the speaker what they just told you. For example, "So your history teacher yelled at the class for ten straight minutes?"

3. **Be honest.** We all have times when we feel super distracted. If it's not a great time for you to listen, go the honesty route. For example, "Mom, I know you need me to do a few things while you're on your conference call, but I'm feeling super distracted and I'm not really paying attention. Can we talk about it in ten minutes after I have a snack and get changed?"

If you answered mostly Bs, you are on the way to being a good listener, but your skills could still use some fine-tuning. Practice the strategies given for the "mostly As" answers, and you will be there in no time.

If you answered mostly Cs, you are a natural listener. Way to go!

Sticky Note Self-Reflection

How did you score on the quiz? Is there anything you should work on? Write it down.

3. Play Up Your Strengths

Sometimes it seems to **Celeste** that everyone except her has something they are good at. Her best friend is an amazing gymnast, her brother is a chess wiz, and two of her other close friends are straight-A students. Celeste feels so "average." Her grades are okay. She's a decent basketball player. What she really enjoys is listening to her friends when they have problems. She always feels good about herself when a friend comes to her with a problem and asks for help in solving it. Her friends tell her she's a great listener and a great friend. But is that a talent?

There are times when ADHD can do a number on your self-esteem. Doubts can creep up on you and negative thinking or excessive worry can lead to self-critical thoughts. It can be easy to start thinking negatively about yourself when you're faced with a challenge, but that type of thinking is not going to help you. Let's take a look at your strengths and see how these can help you in everyday life. Here's a list of common strengths that many people with ADHD possess. Highlight the ones that apply to you and write down what the strength helps you do or what goals it has helped you achieve.

Creative ....

Productive ....

Multitasker ....

Thinks innovatively/outside of the box ....

High energy ....

Enthusiastic ....

Good negotiator

Detail-oriented

Persistent

Thinks strategically

Optimistic

Great problem-solver

Natural leader

Keen sense of observation

Life of the party

Strong moral compass

Compassionate/empathetic

Sticky Note Self-Reflection

What are your best strengths? Did you discover some that you didn't realize you had? Write them down.

4.

I Can't Make a Decision!

Leila is in Bed, Bath & Beyond with her mother. Leila recently repainted her room and she's picking out some things to go with her new design. The problem is, she can't decide on a new bedspread. Leila does a couple of things that help her make the decision. First, she sets up some decision boundaries to help her narrow down the choices. In this case, the boundaries are budget, color, and feel (Leila wants a very soft bedspread). She narrows her choices down to four bedspreads all in the light blue color she loves, but only one is softer than the rest and fits into the budget her mother gave her. Now she has made her decision.

ADHDers can sometimes struggle with decision-making. Whether it's choosing a box of cereal in the cereal aisle, picking out some new fall clothes, or deciding how to celebrate a birthday, having several choices can bring on feelings of anxiety and being overwhelmed.

Let's learn a couple of tricks to minimize the stress of decision-making.

1. **Set boundaries or parameters to narrow down choices and get specific.** Whether it's cereal or clothes, narrow down your choices by setting boundaries. For example, when shopping for clothes, go in with a plan so you don't wind up overspending or buying something you don't need. Think: "I need two pairs of jeans and three long-sleeved shirts."

2. **Set a deadline for deliberation.** Give yourself a deadline to deliberate and stick to it. If you need to make a quick decision, use a timer.

3. **Crowdsource your options.** Consider one or two trusted sources (parent, sibling, friend, etc.) to help you make your decision.

Sticky Note Self-Reflection

Which strategies stood out to you? Write down one that you'll use the next time you have trouble making a decision.

5. I Can't Find Anything in My Room

Juan's room is a mess. He has piles of papers on the floor, clothes hanging off of his desk chair, his mice have escaped, and he can't locate his most important personal belongings. Somewhere in this room are his phone, his wallet, his school ID, and his planner, all of which he needs now.

Look at the picture and use your highlighter to help Juan find the items he needs.

Now let's go over a couple of strategies to help you get and stay organized.

1. **Set up a command center.** You need one central place to put the essentials—such as your phone, wallet, and keys—when you enter your room. By creating the habit of placing the essentials in the command center as soon as you go into

your room, you can quickly find those items whenever you need to. Your command center can be a small shelf with some hooks, a bookshelf with a designated storage cube, or a drawer in your desk or dresser. The key is to make sure it is located near the door to your room. Your command center is the first place you will go when you need one of your essentials.

2. **Get it off the floor.** Installing some well-placed hooks and bookshelves on your walls can help keep the usual culprits (towels, pajamas, sports uniforms, etc.) from cluttering your floor and will also make it easier to find what you need quickly.

3. **Zone your room.** Think of your room as having a couple of separate 'zones' with different purposes. For example, your desk is your workspace/studying area, the chair in the corner is for music or another hobby, and your bed is, well, you know what your bed is for.

4. **Make use of storage containers.** Give pesky, clutter-creating items a home by getting some containers, baskets, or bins that you designate for their purpose. For example, you may have one basket for your sports equipment, one for your sheet music, and one for your graded tests and quizzes.

5. **Enlist the help of a friend.** Do you have a friend whose room is organized to a T and looks right out of Pinterest? Some people have great organizational instincts. Ask your friend for some tips. Maybe they can give you some ideas and help you turn your space into someplace you love to be.

Sticky Note Self-Reflection

What did you learn about your room? Is there any part about it you think could use improvement? Which of these strategies are you excited to try? Write down your ideas here.

6. Where Does the Time Go?

Gabby notices that no matter what she does, she loses track of time and it is starting to really affect her life and relationships—she has been late to school and she has angered her friends by picking them up late for practice. She has noticed that she feels a little panicked and anxious about getting places on time.

It's true that having ADHD can alter your temporal awareness, or sense of time. This isn't necessarily a bad thing. In fact, there are times when you may be able to use it to your advantage. Whatever the case, there are some tools you can use to help yourself keep track of time better.

First, you must use some sort of timer. There are several different types of timers, so let's find the right one for you.

Use music as a timer for short tasks. Gabby knows that she doesn't have a lot of time to shower in the morning. She should take a shower that lasts no longer than 4 minutes. Gabby looks at the favorite songs on her playlist and finds a 4-minute song she can play. When the song is over, her shower is over.

Visual timer. Some people respond better to visual timers rather than aural timers. They find visual timers less stressful and are able to quickly refer to them without getting distracted. Examples of visual timers are the VisTimer, which is a pie-chart timer app, or a sand or hourglass timer.

Second, you must know how to estimate time. ADHDers tend to underestimate how long tasks will take, so it's always better to allow more time for any task. Think of it this way: Wouldn't you far prefer to have time left over than be rushing to finish something?

Sticky Note Self-Reflection

Which time strategy would work best for you? Write down one to try next time you need to be more conscious of keeping time.

7. Sometimes You're a Little Bit Extra

Josh has a big personality. He often gets described as the life of the party, the class clown, and someone with a ton of energy. When he was younger, he had the tendency to sometimes annoy his peers by talking a lot and always trying to get a laugh from his friends. Now that he's older, he notices that these traits appear more in certain situations, such as when he's in large groups of friends, when he's nervous or unsure, or when he's feeling a little out of his element.

For some with ADHD, the struggle with hyperactivity gets easier as they get older. It may have to do with maturity or with the ability to harness energy more easily into sports, hobbies, or work. However, some teens still struggle on a daily basis with their "extra." This may mean you constantly fidget in class; you can't sit still when you are at home; or you talk a little more, a little louder, and a little faster than everyone else. As you get older, hyperactivity can also lead to some damaging habits, such as compulsive spending or online shopping, gaming addiction, and difficulty maintaining friendships and relationships.

Developing your self-awareness is key to preventing your "extra" from getting in your way. Your "extra" tends to show up more in certain situations or when you feel certain emotions.

Know your "extra" symptoms. Your "extra" symptoms are behaviors that exhibit signs of hyperactivity. Highlight the symptoms that apply to you.

- Talking too much
- Interrupting
- Constantly making jokes
- Fidgeting/moving a lot

Know your "extra" triggers. Whereas "extra" symptoms display the behaviors of hyperactivity, triggers are the situations or feelings that cause those symptoms to arise. Highlight your triggers in the list.

- Feeling nervous/anxious
- Being in a large social group
- New situations
- Being excited

Try different calming strategies. Take a walk. Do a short YouTube yoga video. Take a couple of really big deep breaths. Listen to soothing music or sounds from nature such as ocean waves, rainfall, etc. Journaling is another great tool you can use, both as an outlet and also as a place to store information you may want to revisit later.

Highlight the strategies you want to try and write them down here.

Turn your "extra" into a talent. Many ADHDers discover that a symptom of their ADHD helped them harness a talent. For example, if you love telling stories and making others laugh, you may be a natural at acting or writing. Try taking an improv class or a screenwriting class.

Brainstorm here about what hidden talents your "extra" may uncover.

Have a code word that you can share with a trusted friend or parent. Your trusted person can use the code word as a signal to you that you are beginning to enter your "extra" zone.

Write down a code word here.

Sticky Note Self-Reflection

Write down your favorite strategy or strategies to best manage your "extra," and try it out the next time you experience one of your triggers.

8. Worry Like a Champ

Callum worries a lot. He has worried for most of his life. He is always thinking about what's happening next. When he was younger, he would worry about who was picking him up from school, which activity he was going to, and the next fun thing he would be doing. Now that he's older his worries have changed a bit. He wonders: What will tomorrow be like? What if I don't do well on my test? What if none of my friends are in my classes this year? How am I going to pass this AP class I'm taking?

Having ADHD means that your mind sometimes processes information at different rates, and this can lead to you feeling like your mind is racing or stalling at different times. Sometimes that feeling of loss of control leads to feelings of anxiety. The key to getting back into the driver's seat is to first acknowledge when it's happening. The second step is to make a couple of key decisions in order to take control of your worry.

Try this exercise to help feel more in control of your worries. Write down a specific worry. For example, "I have no idea how I'm going to get all my homework done this week."

Now, write down how much you believe in the worry, on a scale from 1 to 10, with 1 meaning you don't believe it at all and 10 meaning you completely believe it.

Now write down all the things you can do to turn the worry into a task.

_____

_____

_____

Now, taking into consideration all the things you can do to turn the worry into a task, restate your worry. For example, "I have a lot of work this week, which sucks, but I have a plan to get it all done. These are the things I can do: make a list of upcoming assignments, set reminders for due dates, and use sticky notes for visual reminders."

_____

_____

_____

Sticky Note Self-Reflection

What types of things do you find yourself worrying about the most? Write them down here.

9. Quiz: Take Your Impulsivity Pulse

Take this short quiz to figure out your impulsivity quotient and learn some new strategies to deal with those quick reactions.

1. **You are in the mall, shopping for a new pair of running shoes. On your way to the shoe store, you pass your favorite clothes store and see a fabulous pair of jeans that you've been wanting. What do you do?**

   a. Run into the store, grab the jeans in your size, and race to the nearest register.

   b. Walk into the store, try the jeans on in your size, and make a mental note of the price so you can figure out if you can budget for a pair this month.

   c. Walk by. Jeans are great but you are on a mission to buy running shoes.

2. **There's a brand-new app that everyone at school is downloading. You recently got into trouble with your parents for downloading apps that cost money, but the temptation is real. What do you do?**

   a. It's already downloading . . .

   b. Check out the app on your friend's phone and figure out a way to convince your parents to let you buy it.

   c. Decide to table the app for right now, because it's just not worth the aggravation.

3. **You are in a huge fight with your sister. She promised to drive you to your best friend's house tonight where the plan is to put on face masks, watch Netflix, and order takeout, but now she has bailed on you because her boyfriend needs her to drive him to his job. Your parents are out for the day and your plan just went down the tubes. What do you do?**

   a. Seek revenge. You know how to embarrass your sister and all it takes is a minute on Snapchat.

b. Try to convince your sister to drive you a little earlier so you can still have your fun night with your best friend.

c. Reschedule with your friend for next week and try to find something on Netflix to distract you from your annoying sister.

4. **You have to take an art class as a requirement for graduation, but you just don't enjoy drawing, plus you don't feel like you have any natural talent. The assignment due tomorrow is a pencil drawing of a fruit bowl. Your first attempt looks like something a four-year-old drew and you feel like giving up. What do you do?**

a. Rip it up and resign yourself to getting a zero on the assignment. There's no point in trying if you're not good at it.

b. Watch a few YouTube videos on drawing and make your best effort. It's no DaVinci but it will do.

c. Settle in for a long night of drawing until your fingers bleed.

5. **It's college application time. When looking for the right college for you, what do you do?**

a. Find out where your closest friends are applying and apply there.

b. Sit down with your parents and discuss your budget and your academic interests and come up with a list that fits those parameters.

c. Go to your college counselor's office and read through every college book and pamphlet she has. You want to make sure you apply to a good mix of reach and safety schools.

If you answered mostly As, you may need to rein in your spontaneity when reacting to emotional situations and making hasty decisions. Here are a couple of strategies to try:

a. Try the 1 minute, 10 minutes, 1 hour rule (1-10-1). If you react quickly to emotional situations, the next time you're faced with one, set a timer for 1 minute and during that minute do nothing but focus on your breathing. Next, set a timer for 10 minutes and during those minutes do something physical, such as taking a walk, taking a shower, or doing a few yoga poses. Finally, wait 1 full hour before responding to the situation. Chances are your reaction will be calmer and more thought out instead of hasty, impulsive, and possibly something you will regret.

b. Ask yourself if your future self will be happy with the decision you are making. Oftentimes, when we react quickly to a situation, it leads to feelings of guilt or regret later. Ask your future self if you're going to be happy with the way you reacted three hours from now. What about tomorrow? A week from now?

c. Make it harder to do or say something you might regret. If it's hard not to react emotionally, try giving your phone to someone else for an hour so you can't shoot off that fiery text, or don't take your credit card with you to the mall if you don't want to buy the jeans you've been eyeing.

If you answered mostly Bs, you are on the right track to using the rational side of your brain. Keep on keeping on.

If you answered mostly Cs, you aren't impulsive but you tend to think a little more negatively and you may not be approaching tasks effectively or with the best frame of mind. Make sure you check out the exercise on page 22 on thinking more positively and the strategies presented on pages 78 and 79 on prioritizing.

Sticky Note Self-Reflection

How did you do on the quiz? What did you learn?

10.

It's all in the List, Baby

Ryan is a senior in high school and he was diagnosed with ADHD in 4th grade. It used to be really hard managing his symptoms and trying to stay on top of school, sports, and keeping up with his friends. He's learned several tools to help him cope, but he's developed one habit in particular that he knows will stay with him forever. He makes a list every day. Every day, after he wakes up, he takes one or two minutes to go over his schedule and he makes a list of everything he would like to get done during the day. Before he goes to bed at night, he reviews the list. It helps him check his progress and make sure he got the most important things done, and he can always move anything that he didn't get done to his list for the next day.

Check out Ryan's list. Highlight the things you think should be priorities in one color and the things that could be moved to tomorrow if he doesn't get to them today in another color.

List for Monday, Sept 10

- Bring soccer cleats to school for game today
- Pack lunch and snacks
- Study for English midterm next week
- Bring home *To Kill a Mock-ingbird* for reading, due tomorrow
- Ask bio teacher to write college recommendation (need in 3 weeks)

- Watch *Stranger Things* season finale
- Finish AP chem lab, due tomorrow
- Finalize Fantasy Football picks for Weds
- Practice guitar
- Orthodontist appt, 3:30 p.m.
- Look for summer job online

Sticky Note Self-Reflection

Make your own list for today. It may help you to begin by thinking about your day in chronological order. Ask yourself, what's happening in the morning? What do I need? What's happening at school today? What do I need?

11.

What's Your Rejection Style?

Take this short quiz to assess how you deal with rejection. The truth is that no one likes being rejected, but there are some tricks that can help you deal with your feelings when it does happen.

1. **You worked really hard to audition for the school play. After rehearsing for weeks, today is the day! The cast list is up—and your name isn't on it. What do you do?**

   a. Immediately burst into tears and spend half the day in the bathroom crying and wondering why these awful things only happen to you.

   b. Utter a string of expletives. The play director has it out for you. This is the last time you will ever audition for a play.

   c. Feel really disappointed. But you notice that next to the cast list is a sign-up sheet for stage crew. That could be interesting and you might learn something, and you'd still get to hang out with the cast. You add your name to the list.

2. **You are trying on some clothes that you just ordered online. Your best friend is over and you can't wait to show her the dress you got for a mutual friend's Sweet Sixteen. You try it on and your friend tells you she doesn't think it's flattering on you. What do you do?**

   a. Feel completely hurt, but she's probably right. If that's what she thinks, then you should just return the dress.

   b. Unleash some critical thoughts about your friend that you've kept on reserve for a moment like this.

   c. Take in your friend's comment and decide to shelve it for a while. She has a very particular sense of style and this dress is definitely not what she would choose. Maybe you should ask a couple of other people for their opinions.

3. **You've recently started a new job at a health food store. You just finished stocking the shelves when your manager comes over and points out that you did it all wrong. What do you do?**

   a. Feel crushed. You spent two hours on this task and she hasn't acknowledged any of your hard work.

   b. Seethe in anger. Start ruminating on bitter thoughts. This manager is out to get you.

   c. Ask her for help. It's a new job; you know there's a learning curve and you are going to make some mistakes.

If you answered mostly As, you are rejection sensitive. This means that you take criticism to heart and you tend to interpret criticism as meaning that there is something inherently bad about you. Make sure to turn to pages 62 and 63 and complete the exercise on finding your strengths.

If you answered mostly Bs, you are also rejection sensitive, but you tend to focus your energy outward by placing blame or focus on others. Try to remember that everyone receives criticism from time to time from teachers, friends, parents, and bosses. It's completely normal to not like hearing it; however, finding a way to "hear" and accept criticism is important. Turn to page 76 and practice the 1-10-1 rule to reduce acting impulsively when you feel threatened by criticism.

If you answered mostly Cs, you have found a way to normalize receiving criticism or rejection.

Sticky Note Self-Reflection

What did you learn from the quiz? Write down anything you need to work on.

12. Meditation Station

Sometimes the hardest part about having ADHD is the inability to slow your mind down. At times it may seem as though your brain is racing or thinking about several different things all at once. How can you learn to slow it down so you feel less rushed, your brain feels less crowded, and you can focus on one thing at a time? One proven strategy is to incorporate some mindfulness and meditation into your routine.

What exactly is meditation? Meditation is a practice of focusing your mind on something to achieve a state of calm and clarity—in other words, mindfulness. This may seem impossible to do in the moment. But by practicing slowly, you can gradually increase your ability to slow down your mind.

1. **Try engaging your senses.** Set a timer for one minute. Stop wherever you are. Notice one thing you can look at. Identify one sound you can listen to. Breathe in through your nose and identify what you smell. Put your hands on something near you and focus on the sensation. Take a sip of water and notice the temperature as you swallow.

2. **Try an app such as Headspace, Calm, or Insight Timer.** These all offer short meditations that will get you feeling zen in no time.

3. **Focus on your breathing.** Set a timer for one minute. Practice taking deep breaths in through your nose and out through your mouth. Notice whether you are calmer before or after the exercise.

Sticky Note Self-Reflection

Write down a meditation strategy you plan to try this week. Don't forget to put a reminder on your phone or calendar.

PART FOUR

Q&A: ADHD IN REAL LIFE

IN THIS SECTION

I'd like to talk to you as if you were sitting in my office. There are certain issues and scenarios that tend to come up repeatedly for teens with ADHD, and while you are all unique and have different problems, it's important to know that you aren't alone and there is most likely someone else who is going through whatever you are going through. I'm right here, so let's go through it together.

Q: Today was my third day late to first-period English. I have been having a hard time with the homework and if I show up late, I avoid having to turn in the assignment I didn't do. If I'm late one more time, I receive a detention and my parents get called. My parents and my teacher are already on my case for not keeping up with my homework. What should I do?

A: It sounds like things are piling up at school and you are feeling pretty overwhelmed. Tempting as it may be to hide this from your parents and your teacher, you need to sit down with them and be honest about what is currently giving you difficulty. When you feel overwhelmed, it can seem as though everything is crashing down around you, but a good way to avoid feeling like this is to pinpoint specific problems that you may be able to work on.

Try this: Write down specifically what is hard about getting your English homework done. Here are some questions/prompts that may help you:

Are you struggling with the concepts? If so, you may need to speak to your teacher about extra help after class or working with a tutor.

Are you having a hard time focusing? If this is the case, you may want to talk to your parents about what can be done to help, and don't forget to check out the exercises on pages 32 and 82.

Are you having a hard time writing or getting your ideas onto paper? Try using a mind map (see page 39) or working with a writing tutor.

Once you have your answer, sit down with your parents and let them know what is going on. Reach out to your teacher and share your concerns. Ask your parents and teacher to help you develop a plan to get back on track.

Q: Since I started high school, my supposed best friend started hanging out with some new friends. She doesn't invite me out when she is with them and recently she doesn't even say hi to me in the hallway. I feel really hurt and rejected.

A: It's really painful when someone you care about seems to move on without you. Feeling hurt and rejected is completely normal. It's important to make sure that you have someone to talk to. Here are some things to remember:

High school is a time of transition and experimentation. Your friend may be trying out a new group of friends, and she may not intentionally be ignoring you but may just be rather swept up in the excitement. Consider talking to her about how you feel during a quiet moment alone with her.

Reevaluate your support network. While no one likes feeling left in the dust, you can make some changes to help lessen the pain. Is there a new activity you can join? Are there other friends you can spend more time with?

Think of your friendship like a bank account. You should both be making deposits and withdrawals to keep your friendship healthy. If it feels like a friendship is draining you and only makes you feel negative feelings, it may be time to reevaluate your investment in it.

Q: My parents are mad at me for constantly lying to them. Last night, I promised them I would clean up my room but I didn't, and when they asked what I got on my Latin test I told them I got an A when I really got a D. My mom says my first instinct is to lie and I think deep down she is right. Sometimes I make up lies to cover up other lies that I've told them. Why do I do this?

A: It can be tempting to tell people (especially your parents) what they want to hear, even if it's not the truth. No one wants to give bad or disappointing news or admit to our own shortcomings. The problem with lying is that it's not a solution to a problem and lying will only make things worse.

Here are some questions to help you understand why you may be avoiding the truth.

- Are you worried about getting criticism or disappointing someone?

- Will telling the truth get you into trouble?

- Are you avoiding something you are having difficulty with (such as a long-term project that you don't know how to start or studying for a test you don't feel hopeful about)?

- Do you feel like your parents' expectations are too high for you?

By paying more attention to the worries or concerns that lead you to lie about something, it may help you realize why you resort to bending the truth. Work on solving those problems and eventually you will feel more comfortable speaking the truth.

Q: I'm so sick of all the drama with friends at school. It feels like I never get a break from it. Even when we leave school, everyone is texting or on social media. I don't even enjoy using my phone, but I feel like I have to pay attention to stay on top of what's happening. Sometimes, when I get in trouble with my parents, I'm relieved when they take away my phone because having it can be stressful.

A: Being a teenager now is way different than when your parents were teenagers. Having 24-hour access to everyone in your social network can feel overwhelming and suffocating at times. Wanting to take a break is completely normal and can be really healthy for your brain and your emotional health. Give yourself permission to take a vacation from your phone. Use one of the apps we discussed earlier in this book (see pages 46 and 47) to block social media on your phone if you feel like it's getting in the way of your work. The best way to take a break from social media is to spend some time in nature. Go for a hike or a walk, write in a journal, listen to some music, or spend some time near water.

Q: I usually have a smile on my face and my friends say that I always make them laugh. I get invited to parties and I'm doing okay in school. But lately, I feel very lonely and empty and like no one truly knows me. Sometimes I can go to really dark places in my thoughts. Why do I feel so down and empty? Is there something wrong with me?

A: Everyone feels sad and down at times, but if you feel as though your sadness is getting worse, it's time to reach out for help. There is support out there and acknowledging how you feel is the first step. Talk to someone you trust, such as a school counselor or your parents. Feeling down and depressed can get worse and can lead to more serious thoughts. Consider asking for professional help. If you feel suicidal, contact the National Suicide Prevention hotline at 1-800-273-8255.

Q: My friend asked me if I would give him a couple of my ADHD pills so he could study better for finals. It doesn't seem like a huge deal. Should I do it?

A: This may not initially seem like a big deal, but sharing a prescribed medicine (especially a controlled substance, such as a stimulant) can have very serious consequences if someone they weren't prescribed for takes them. Keep in mind that your friend may have a medical condition you don't know about that would make taking your medicine very dangerous. Also, he doesn't have ADHD. You do. Think about it this way: If you had a heart condition and your friend asked you to give him one or two of your heart pills, would you do it? Probably not. Sharing your medicine is never a good idea. If you want to help your friend, show them some of the studying and focusing strategies you have learned in this book. If your friend is concerned that they have ADHD, encourage them to speak to their parents or doctor about it.

Q: Everyone is taking the SATs this year and my teachers and parents will not stop talking about it. I do terrible with standardized tests and this one seems so important. It feels like I won't get into college unless I do well and I feel like I'm going to bomb. Should I still take the tests?

A: There's a lot of pressure to do well on the standardized tests used for college entrance. It's normal to feel anxious and worried about taking them. First of all, make sure you check out the exercise for test-taking anxiety (page 23). Next, talk to your school counselor about whether your diagnosis of ADHD qualifies you for any accommodations, such as extra time. This may help ease your worries about the exam. Also, keep in mind that there are a huge variety of colleges out there. It is true that some colleges focus heavily on SAT scores, but many schools weigh other accomplishments more heavily, such as grades, extracurricular activities, and community involvement.

Q: I tried vaping at a party a few weeks ago and ever since then I've wanted to do it again. I know my parents would be furious if they found out. But it's healthier than smoking, right? What's the big deal if I get my own JUUL?

A: Here are some great reasons not to start vaping:

- There are very high levels of nicotine in a JUUL. One pod can have more nicotine than a pack of cigarettes.

- It can have serious health consequences. Studies coming out now about vaping are showing that they can cause serious lung irritation, and JUUL pods have carcinogenic (cancer-causing) materials in them.

- It can impact your athletic abilities. Vaping causes blood circulation issues by raising your heart rate and impairing blood vessel function.

- Vaping is highly addictive and can greatly impact your ability to focus.

Now that you've learned some of the negative consequences of vaping, does it still seem like it's not a big deal? Try to be honest with yourself about why you want to do it. Is it about fitting in? Did you like the way it made you feel? Make a list of all the negative and positive consequences that vaping would have on your life if it became a habit. It's natural to want to experiment with new things when you are a teenager, but making something a habit can have some more serious consequences and may not be worth it in the end.

Q: I used to get in trouble all the time when I was younger. Now that I'm older and doing better, I feel like people—especially my friends' parents—still think I'm a "bad kid." It feels like I won't ever be able to shake that reputation. How can I change what people think about me?

A: ADHD plays out very differently in childhood than it does in your teenage years. It can feel unfair to still be judged by the way you conducted yourself when you were seven years old. It's also true that some people may believe myths or stereotypes about ADHD. They may be stuck in their own thinking, which doesn't allow room for others to change. The bottom line is that you have to become your own advocate. You know that you have come a long way. The best way to change other people's perception of you is to keep working on you and spend as little time as possible worrying about what others think.

Q: While I was in the middle of a couple of group texts, I accidentally sent a text about my friend *to her*. It was really mean and now I feel awful. She isn't speaking to me and now she's blocked me on social media. What should I do?

A: Once a text, tweet, or Snapchat is sent, it's out there and, until we can learn how to time travel, it can't get taken back. It can feel awful when you shared something you now regret sharing, or in this case, sent something hurtful to someone you care about. Here are a few things to keep in mind.

- Give your friend a little space. She's angry, and she has a right to feel that way. Reaching out to her right away may not be the best strategy. Put yourself in her shoes. If the roles were reversed, would you want to talk right away?

- After some time has passed, ask to speak to her in person. You will better be able to convey your apology if your friend can see you face-to-face. Attempting to talk about the situation through texting could further muddy the waters.

- Keep it between you and your friend. Try not to let others get involved in what happened. You made a mistake, but it's your mistake, so it won't help to have other friends chime in or try to help you by talking to your friend.

Q: I feel as though whenever I start something new, like a new school year or a new athletic season, I start out with the best intentions. I think to myself, "I'm going to get on the honor roll" or "I'm going to get nominated for MVP," but I always end up making the same mistakes. I'm late, I forget about important things (like homework or practices), and then I just get frustrated with myself. Will I ever be able to change?

A: It can feel good to mark the start of something new with a bold statement, such as "Everything is going to be different." "This year I'm going to do all my homework as soon as I get home." However, making statements like these without making a plan for how to accomplish what you intend can make it very difficult for you to reach your goals. Let's say your goal is to make the honor roll. Think of three things that got in the way of you achieving this in the past. Examples might be: not turning in homework on time, forgetting about assignments, and not taking advantage of extra credit assignments. Now make a plan for how to fix these three things. The plan might look like this:

1. Start a homework routine to check assignments every night before bed.

2. Ask a trusted friend or source to be your "homework buddy" to hold you accountable for completing assignments.

3. Find out extra credit due dates and put reminders on your calendar so you don't miss those opportunities.

Making small behavioral changes will get you the best bang for your buck when it comes to maintaining consistent change. Continue to use all the strategies you have learned in this workbook, set reminders, and make lists. Think of yourself as a work in progress that you are continually striving to improve. You are the Editor in Chief of *The Life and Times of You*!

Q: I have trouble sleeping during the week. I stay up late talking to my friends, then I start homework, and by the time I'm done it's midnight or 1 a.m. My alarm goes off at 5:45 a.m. and I feel like a zombie when I get up. What can I do?

A: Many teens struggle with getting enough sleep. Teenage brains are wired to be more active in the evenings, so it's not uncommon that you just don't feel tired when it might be time to go to bed. However, consistently not getting enough sleep can lead to feeling groggy, unfocused, and cranky and you may be tempted to take a nap after school, which may further disrupt your sleep later, and so the cycle continues. Here are a few strategies to try.

1. Make changes in 30-minute intervals. Suddenly starting to go to bed two or three hours earlier is jarring for your body and your brain. Instead, try adjusting your bedtime slowly by 30-minute intervals each week or every few days. This will give your body time to adjust and it will be easier for you to fall asleep at a reasonable hour.

2. Try to limit social media, phone, and computer use right before going to bed. I know this one is hard but it could make all the difference. The blue light emitted from electronics sends a signal to the brain to stay awake, which can really make falling and staying asleep very challenging.

3. Create a relaxing bedtime routine. Our bodies crave routine, especially with sleep habits. Try to create a calming routine that sends the signal to your brain that you are getting very sleepy. Turn the lights down. Read a book. Put on some soothing sounds or music. Do a quick bedtime meditation. Have a cup of chamomile tea. Incorporate this behavior into your daily bedtime ritual.

Q: I recently started talking to a guy I really like. I had a crush on him at school for the longest time and now he is paying more attention to me. Last night, he "sexted" me a picture of himself and asked me to send him one back. I really like this guy but I feel really uncomfortable. What should I do?

A: Sexting is common among teens, but just because it's commonplace doesn't mean it's something you have to do. It's also really important to remember that a recent study by the Internet Watch Foundation found that 88 percent of self-generated images have been collected and shared on different websites. Once you send someone a picture of yourself, it's gone, and you have no control over what is done with that image.

According to Common Sense Media, there are some very important "what ifs" to keep in mind when you are considering sending an image of yourself via text:

- What if your relationship status changes?

- What if someone else scrolls through the other person's phone and sees your image?

- What if a parent checks your phone and sees the image?

- What if the person loses their phone?

- What if they change their mind?

Check out Common Sense Media at CommonSenseMedia.org for more tips on how to turn down a sext request.

Q: I have a group history project and I got placed with a few of my friends, which I initially thought was great. The problem is every time we get together to work on the project, we start laughing and fooling around. We haven't gotten any work done and I'm afraid to be the one to say something. What should I do?

A: No one wants to be that person—the one who stops the fun with a reality check on what you are supposed to be doing. But you also don't want to be the one who does poorly on your group project. What's the best way to address a situation like this without feeling as though you are the boring friend?

First, remind yourself that these people are your friends. Chances are that you have common goals and doing well in school is probably one of those goals. Second, take a stab at being a leader. Maybe you have a great idea the group could get started on. Try approaching one of your friends individually, so when you bring it up to the group, you have support.

Q: I feel like I get bored so easily. I get really excited when I start a new activity or a new club but then I lose interest quickly. Will I ever find something that I love and I'm passionate about?

A: Boredom is not uncommon for ADHDers. Let's dig a little deeper and figure out what your "boredom" means. The term can be an umbrella for some more specific feelings or emotions. For some, boredom is triggered when things get challenging or frustrating. If this is the case, it's important to be honest with yourself about what you are feeling. Use some honest self-talk, such as "I think I'm feeling bored, but I'm actually frustrated that I can't master this."

For others, the feeling of boredom arises during routines or busy work. ADHDers love that dopamine hit when things are exciting, new, and even risky. In this case, try a self-talk statement such as "It's boring to do this right now, but it's helping me sharpen my skills. I know I can push through it."

Q: I just lost my third phone. My parents told me that if I want a new phone, I have to buy my own. How can I stop losing important things?

A: Losing expensive things such as phones can be stressful. First, let's look at some of the behaviors that might be contributing to losing your phone.

- Do you always keep your phone in the same place? Keeping it in a jacket or pocket is a great way to lose it. Jackets get taken off and phones can easily fall out of pockets.

- What are you not losing? Have you kept your backpack all year? If so, then maybe this is where your phone needs to live.

- Enlist the help of a buddy. Ask a trusted friend to remind you to check if you have your phone after practice or before you leave an after-school activity.

Q: My parents are divorced and I sometimes find it really hard to go back and forth between their houses. I feel disorganized, unfocused, and anxious when I have to remember everything I need to stay at the other parent's place. Sometimes, I just wish I could stay in one place. I don't want to tell my parents this because I know it will upset them.

A: This is a tough situation. Having ADHD is hard enough, but the stressors of having to move between two households can make it even harder. While I know you don't want to upset your parents, speaking to them about your concerns may actually be very helpful. Perhaps you could brainstorm with your parents different systems of communication or traveling that could minimize your feelings of anxiety. Most likely your parents are going to understand and will want to support you to do the best that you can.

Q: I just started high school and I'm completely overwhelmed. My new school is so much bigger than my middle school and the teachers expect so much more. They are already talking about college and I practically just graduated 8th grade.

A: The move to high school can feel like you went from a small pond to a huge ocean. Feeling overwhelmed is normal, especially with so much emphasis being placed on the future. Try to allow yourself to be in the moment and enjoy some of the small joys of high school: You have more independence. You can meet new friends and try new classes/sports/activities. You are going to be treated differently. The best way to conquer feeling overwhelmed at a new school is to get more information. Make sure you find out if there is a mentoring program at your high school. Having an upperclassman to talk to or show you the ropes can be super helpful. Talk to your guidance counselor. Get a list of all of the clubs, activities, and sports offered and figure out one or two that you may want to try.

Q: I'm a senior in high school, and after discussing it at length with my parents, I think I should wait a year to start college because I'm just not feeling quite ready for it yet. I'm thinking about getting a job and taking a couple of community college classes. Part of me thinks this is the right plan for me and part of me feels like a failure. All of my friends are going to college straightaway, and I know I'm going to feel lonely and left out when they leave. How can I feel better about this?

A: It's hard to be the one person who chooses a slightly different path. It may feel like you are falling behind or not keeping up, but as you said—this is the right plan for you. Not every person is going to go away to college right away and not every person is going to go to college. Finding the best plan for you after high school is the best thing you can do. It's harder to take a left turn when everyone else has their right blinker on, but you may find that you learn and grow immensely in the next year. Take some time to commend yourself for knowing what you need.

Q: Sometimes I have horrible anger outbursts. It's usually toward my parents when I've had a bad day or when I've let things build up inside me. I feel horrible after lashing out at them but I don't know how to stop it from happening. Recently it got so bad that I cursed out my teammate at tennis practice and threw my racket across the court. My coach pulled me aside and told me I need to find a way to chill out. What can I do?

A: It's common for people with ADHD to feel out of control of their emotions at times. Angry outbursts can have lasting negative effects on both you and the people around you who experience them. You may start to develop negative feelings about yourself, and having intense anger episodes can strain relationships with those you love. There are a few things you should keep in mind as you work on this issue.

- Know your triggers. Many people have "triggers" or particular stressors—which may be situations or feelings—that cause these outbursts. See if you can identify a pattern. This will help you plan better for when those situations arise.

- Practice deep breathing. Have you ever noticed that when you get really angry your face gets red, you feel short of breath, and your heart rate increases? These are all signs that your body isn't taking in enough oxygen, which sends your body into "fight or flight" mode. Practice deep breathing at the first sign of frustration by taking long deep breaths in through your nose and out through your mouth.

- Develop some extra outlets during periods of high stress. If you know that you are more likely to "melt down" during busy weeks when you have a ton of homework, make sure you schedule time to do something relaxing you enjoy, such as exercising, going for a hike, or planning a coffee outing with a friend.

- Give yourself a time-out. We all need to step away from certain situations at times in order to get some perspective and allow ourselves to feel calmer. Sometimes a change in environment (even if it's as simple as walking into a different room) can de-escalate angry feelings.

- Dig deep. Anger is an "easy" feeling to show. Just think of all the angry drama on reality TV shows. Men especially can feel that it's the emotion they are "allowed" and even expected to show. But oftentimes there are other emotions pushing that anger up. You may notice that when you have an outburst you are actually feeling vulnerable, ashamed, embarrassed, or hurt. Reach out to a counselor or ask to speak to a therapist if you feel like you need more help dealing with your emotions.

Q: I'm constantly fighting with my parents about playing video games. They seem to hate it when I play and they put all sorts of limits on it. They don't understand that it's the one thing that helps me relax and feel normal. Is gaming really that bad?

A: Playing video games isn't all bad. In fact, there are some benefits to playing video games, such as strengthening hand-eye coordination. Your parents may be worried about you becoming addicted to video games, which can have some negative consequences, including risks of depression and anxiety. You likely enjoy playing because most people enter into a state of "hyper focus" when they play, which for people with ADHD can feel very relaxing.

Try sitting down to talk to your parents about your gaming. Ask them to play with you so you can show them what you enjoy. Explain to them what your feelings are and listen to them when they express their concerns. You may be able to come to a compromise that will help make it less of a hot topic in your home.

Q: I'm supposed to start driving lessons soon and I'm really anxious about it. I'm worried about getting distracted and staying focused. What if I can't do it? What if I get into an accident?

A: The first time practicing driving causes anxiety for most people. It's a completely new situation and it may feel like there are too many things to think about simultaneously. However, just like riding a bicycle, driving will get easier each time you do it and then suddenly it will all come together. In order to reduce your anxiety in the meantime, make sure to keep yourself busy before driving lessons. Practice positive thinking: Instead of thinking of every-thing that could go wrong, picture yourself in the driver's seat feeling completely in control. Imagine the sense of independence that driving can bring.

Q: Whenever I have a problem at school, my parents always step in. They are constantly monitoring my grades and they know when I've missed assignments. Last year, they emailed my English teacher without telling me and asked her if I could get extra help. I had already asked her myself. How can I get my parents to back off?

A: It can be difficult for parents of teenagers to know when to loosen the reins a little. Parents of kids with ADHD have to become advocates for their kids (especially in their younger years) to make sure they get the support they need at school and to help them navigate issues with friends and activities. They may not realize that you are ready to be your own advocate. Try sitting down with your parents and explaining how you feel. Most likely your parents will be thrilled to hear that you want to be more independent. If your parents are more reluctant to loosen their hold on you, try to slowly engage them in a compromise. Make a list of the things you are doing to become more independent. Show them what you have learned by reading this book. Try listening to their concerns, and suggest ways that you could meet in the middle.

Q: Why is it so hard for me to admit I'm wrong? My parents and my friends have all told me that I can never admit I'm wrong, and I'm starting to think they are right. Why can't I just own up to my mistakes?

A: Let's face it: no one likes to admit to being wrong. And having ADHD can sometimes make it even harder. Why? There could be a few reasons, but one may be that children with ADHD get much more negative feedback than other children. Over the course of time, you may have built in a defense mechanism against this. After all, if you don't admit to it, it's not your problem. But as much as you may not like it, being able to own up to your faults is a valuable skill in building personal and professional relationships.

So, what can you do about learning to admit when you're wrong? Well, you've already taken a huge first step by acknowledging that this is an issue you would like to work on. A great way to address it is through journaling. Keeping a regular journal can give you valuable information and insights about yourself. The next time you feel blamed for something, write about it before you react to it. See if this small act creates a change or shift in your thinking.

Q: Will ADHD always make my life hard? Will this ever get easier?

A: The quick answer to this question is that ADHD will always make your life different. Some things will be harder, yes. However, if you choose to view having ADHD through a positive lens, the possibilities are endless. You have unique qualities, strengths, and talents. Your brain is wired differently, but as a result you have become a master electrician. You have become your own advocate, you have learned new skills and strategies, you have built strength, and you have grit. By reading this book and completing the exercises within it, you have become an expert on your ADHD.

You've made it to the end of this workbook. That is a *huge* deal. First of all, I want to congratulate you on all your hard work. You have learned new skills, strategies, and tricks to help you at school, home, work, and beyond. You should also feel better equipped to tackle any sticky situations that come up and feel more confident as a young person with ADHD out in the world. Remember your strengths—they will take you far in any situation. Be sure to make a date every month or so to revisit what you have learned. Keep using your sticky note self-reflections. You have ADHD and you are better for it. Go on and live your best ADHD life.

RESOURCES

Resources *for* Teens

Websites

ADDitudeMag.com

CHADD.org

CommonSenseMedia.org

CrisisTextline.org

GoAskAlice.Columbia.edu

TheTrevorProject.org

Hashtags

#ADHDprobs

#onein15m

Books

Atomic Habits
   by James Clear

Smart but Scattered Teens
   by Richard Guare,
   Peg Dawson and
   Colin Guare

Products

Bullet Journal

Graphic organizers: Understood.org

Mind Map Software:
   matchware.com

Podcasts

ADHD reWired by Eric Tivers

ADHD Support Talk Radio

TED Talks

I Have ADHD, What is Your
   Superpower? by Negar
   (Nikki) Amini

This is what it's really like to live
   with ADHD by Jessica McCabe

YouTube Channels

How to ADHD

Apps

Calm

CHADD

Cold Turkey

Due

Evernote

Freedom

Google Calendar

Google Keep

Google Tasks

Headspace

Hocus Focus

IFTTT (If This Then That)

Insight Timer

OFFTIME

Remind Me

RescueTime

VisTimer

Resources *for* Parents

Websites

ADDitudeMag.com (check out the free webinars for parents)

CHADD.org

CommonSenseMedia.org

LDAAmerica.org/parents

LivesInTheBalance.org

ParentsMedGuide.org

Understood.org

Books

Boy Without Instructions
  by Penny Williams

The Explosive Child
  by Ross W. Greene

Podcasts

Parenting ADHD
  Podcast by Penny Williams

Parenting Your Challenging Child
  Podcast by Ross W. Greene

The ADHD Mama
  Podcast with Susy Parker

TED Talks

Making ADHD Your Superpower
  by George Cicci

Your Child's Most Annoying Trait
  May Reveal Their Greatest
  Strengths by Josh Shipp

REFERENCES

Barkley, Russell A. (2015). *Etiologies of ADHD*. In R. A. Barkley (Ed.).

Attention-Deficit Hyperactivity Disorder: A Handbook for Diagnosis and Treatment, 4th ed. (pp. 356–390). New York, NY: Guilford Press.

https://www.additudemag.com/study-music-to-focus-the-adhd-brain

https://chadd.org/wp-content/uploads/2018/05/managing_medication.pdf

https://www.psychologytoday.com/us/blog/changepower/201704/how -do-work-breaks-help-your-brain-5-surprising-answers

https://www.colorcom.com/research/why-color-matters

iwf.org.uk/sites/default/files/inline-files/IWF_study_self_generated _content_online_011112.pdf

Pastor, Patricia N. (August 28, 2015). QuickStats: Percentage of Children and Adolescents Aged 5–17 Years with Diagnosed Attention-Deficit/ Hyperactivity Disorder (ADHD), by Race and Hispanic Ethnicity—National Health Interview Survey, United States, 1997–2014, *Morbidity and Mortality Weekly Report (MMWR)* 64(33):925–925.

INDEX

ABOUT THE AUTHOR

Allison K. Tyler, LCSW, is a licensed clinical social worker who has specialized in working with children, teens, and adults with ADHD over the course of her sixteen-year career. She graduated from New York University with her Master of Social Work degree in 2003; has a postgraduate certificate in Children and Families from Royal Holloway University in London, United Kingdom; and has a BA from Colby College.

Allison works in private practice and has developed a unique skills-based approach that she individualizes for each of her clients. When working with children and teens, Allison works in partnership with parents, and she also provides parent training and consultation services to schools. Allison has completed Ross Greene's advanced level training in collaborative problem-solving and incorporates the tenets of Dr. Greene's philosophy into all her clinical work.

Allison lives in New Jersey with her loving and very British husband, Jonathan; their son, Callum; daughter, Celeste; and their labradoodle, Ivy.

CPSIA information can be obtained
at www.ICGtesting.com
Printed in the USA
JSHW030012251021
19826JS00003B/3